The Metal Detective

by Linda Lott
illustrated by Nicole Wong

Scott Foresman
is an imprint of

PEARSON

Glenview, Illinois • Boston, Massachusetts • Chandler, Arizona
Upper Saddle River, New Jersey

Every effort has been made to secure permission and provide appropriate credit for photographic material. The publisher deeply regrets any omission and pledges to correct errors called to its attention in subsequent editions.

Unless otherwise acknowledged, all photographs are the property of Pearson.

Photo locations denoted as follows: Top (T), Center (C), Bottom (B), Left (L), Right (R), Background (Bkgd)

Illustrations by Nicole Wong

Photograph 12 Omni-Photo Communications, Inc.

ISBN 13: 978-0-328-51375-8
ISBN 10:   0-328-51375-X

Copyright © by Pearson Education, Inc., or its affiliates. All rights reserved.
Printed in the United States of America. This publication is protected by copyright, and permission should be obtained from the publisher prior to any prohibited reproduction, storage in a retrieval system, or transmission in any form or by any means, electronic, mechanical, photocopying, recording, or likewise. For information regarding permissions, write to Pearson Curriculum Rights & Permissions, One Lake Street, Upper Saddle River, New Jersey 07458.

Pearson® is a trademark, in the U.S. and/or in other countries, of Pearson plc or its affiliates.

Scott Foresman® is a trademark, in the U.S. and/or in other countries, of Pearson Education, Inc., or its affiliates.

3 4 5 6 7 8 9 10 V0N4 13 12 11 10

Joe had been so bored earlier that day that he had tied and untied his shoelaces in different ways. Luckily, his grandmother had invited him over to visit. Now Joe was sitting with her on her porch and drinking lemonade.

Grandma's neighbor, Ms. Choi, was visiting too. Suddenly Joe saw something on the porch that he hadn't seen before.

"What's that?" Joe asked.

"That's my metal detector," Grandma answered. "Here, I'll show you and Ms. Choi how to use it."

Joe and Ms. Choi watched as Grandma turned on the machine. "It's fun," she said. "When it beeps, I know a metal object is hiding below. Then I search until I find it."

"Wow!" said Joe. "May I try it later?"
Knowing that Joe liked to collect coins, Grandma said, "Of course you may! You might find a few coins for your collection!"

They all sat down on Grandma's porch again. "Whew!" Ms. Choi said. "I love my big garden, but caring for it is a lot of work." She reached for her lemonade but stopped suddenly. She looked upset.

There was a strain in her voice as she spoke. "I've lost my special ring," she cried. "It belonged to my grandmother. It must have fallen into my garden!"

"Don't worry, Ms. Choi," Joe said. "I'll find your ring for you!"

Joe quickly realized that he had taken on an enormous task. Ms. Choi's whole yard was a garden! Joe needed more information to narrow his search. "Where were you working?" he asked.

"Everywhere!" explained Ms. Choi. "The ring will be too hard to find, Joe!"

Then Joe and Grandma had an idea. Joe ran for the metal detector.

He searched the flowerbeds and watched two butterflies. Then the machine beeped, and he dug up bent nails.

Next, Joe looked in the bushes. The machine beeped again. This time, Joe happily picked up some scattered coins.

Joe kept trying. The machine beeped a third time. Joe gently parted the ivy that covered the ground. Suddenly he spotted something shiny. It was a gold ring!

Joe ran over and handed the ring to Ms. Choi. "Oh, thank you!" she said. "I'm going to give you a reward, Joe!"

"You've already given me my reward," Joe said. "You helped me decide how to keep myself busy this summer. I'm going to be a metal detector detective!"

Before You Go Out Searching

Using a metal detector can be a fun hobby. Before you go out metal detecting, though, there are some rules you must learn to follow.

Metal detectors are not allowed on National Park Service lands. Those places include national sea coasts, federal parks, historic battlefields and markers, and Native American burial grounds. Also, there are many other places, such as public schools, churches, and private lands, where you must ask permission before you use a metal detector.

If you're ever in doubt about whether you can use a metal detector, just ask! You can also go onto the Internet and look for information about groups that use metal detectors. Happy searching!